C000244054

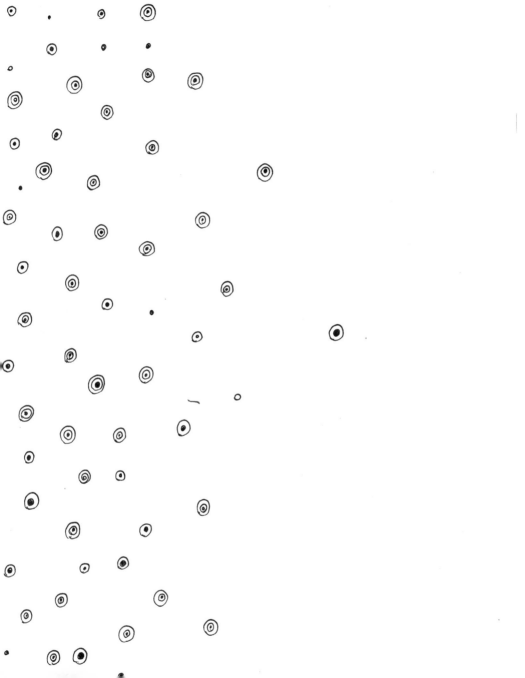

Handwritten Notes to My Friend

Handwritten Notes to My Friend

hardie grant books
MELBOURNE · LONDON

in assocation with PQ Blackwell

forever

I have spent some of
the happiest moments
of my life with you.
... I love being friends
with you.

HeRe's a
BIG HUG
FROM Me, to
SHoW I CaRe
anD You're IN
my thoughts
EVeN WHeN
I Can't Be tHeRe

XO

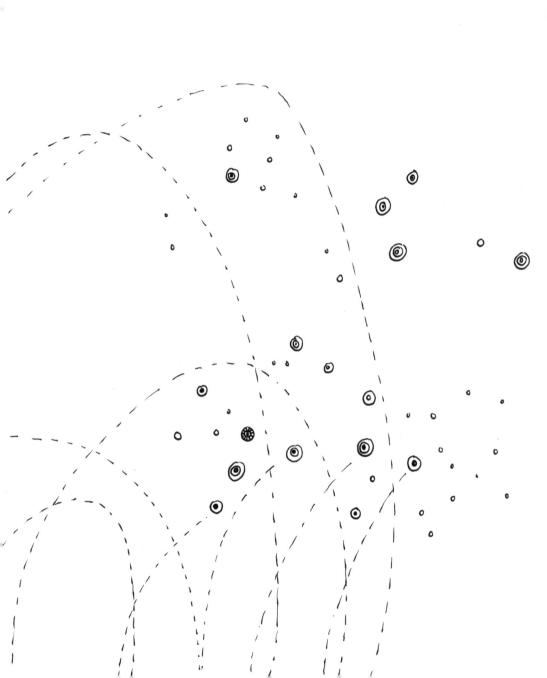

BEING YOUR FRIEND IS EXCITING.
YOU EMBRACE LIFE WITH SO MUCH ENTHUSIASM
AND ARE ALWAYS UP FOR ANYTHING NO MATTER WHAT.
TELL ME, DO YOU EVER RUN OUT OF ENERGY,
OR DO YOU POSSESS SOME KIND
OF SUPERPOWER?

I overheard some people talking about you the other day. They were talking about what a unique and interesting person you are, how you're so warm and friendly and always make people feel good about themselves. I agree with them.

i can't wait to see you again.
i keep imagining the places we'll go
and the conversations we'll have.
Hurry up and CALL ME!

⋅ ⋅ ✦ ⋅ ⋅

Wherever we go
and whatever life sends
I know we'll always be
the BEST of FRIENDS

⋅ ⋅ ✦ ⋅ ✦ ⋅ ✦ ⋅ ✦ ⋅ ⋅ ⋅

⋅ ⋅ ✦ ⋅ ⋅

YAY
FOR BEING
BEST FRIENDS
WITH YOU

YOU'RE THE BEE'S KNEES
(BEES HAVE AMAZING KNEES)

Remember
The path is not straight
Mistakes need not be fatal

whenever I finish a good book,
I immediately want to take it over
to your house and demand that you
read it on the spot so we can discuss it
    in great detail.
Your opinion means so much to me

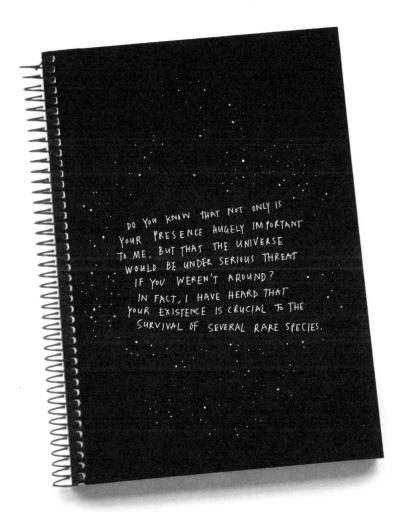

DO YOU KNOW THAT NOT ONLY IS
YOUR PRESENCE HUGELY IMPORTANT
TO ME, BUT THAT THE UNIVERSE
WOULD BE UNDER SERIOUS THREAT
IF YOU WEREN'T AROUND?
IN FACT, I HAVE HEARD THAT
YOUR EXISTENCE IS CRUCIAL TO THE
SURVIVAL OF SEVERAL RARE SPECIES.

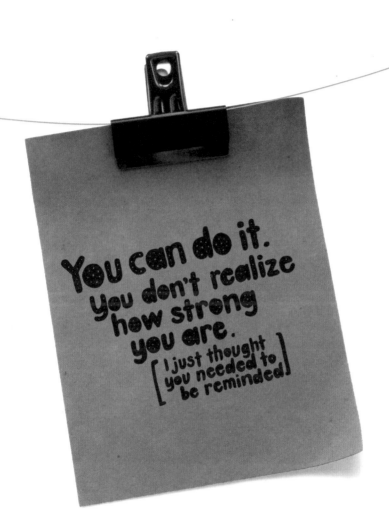

I am YOUR
FRIEND

I am your friend... :)

I am YOUR
friend

I am
your
friend :)

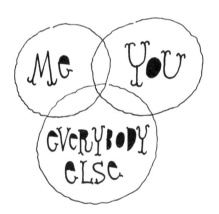

THANKS

...for reminding me that the world is a wonderful place with so much fun to be had.

YOU'RE A TRUE FRIEND.
HOW MANY TIMES HAVE YOU LISTENED
TO ME POUR MY HEART OUT TO YOU?
YOU'RE ALWAYS THERE FOR ME.
I'M SO GRATEFUL FOR THAT.
ALL MY LOVE...AND MELODRAMA.
YOUR FRIENDSHIP IS SUCH A COMFORT TO ME.

MY DEAR
FRIEND
———
THINKING
OF YOU

I SAW A RAINBOW TODAY, AND IT REMINDED ME OF YOU, A COLOURFUL CONTRIBUTION TO THE WORLD

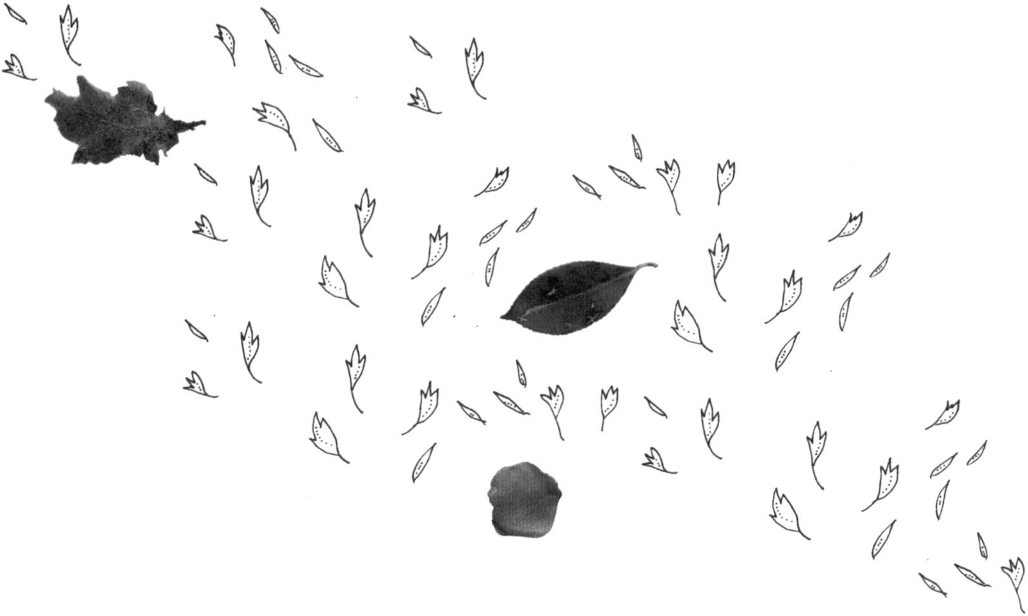

A WALK THROUGH THE WOODS
WITH YOU ON A SUNNY DAY
   IS THE PERFECT TONIC
   FOR MY SPIRITS.
SO PUT ON YOUR SENSIBLE
WALKING SHOES
      AND JOIN ME.

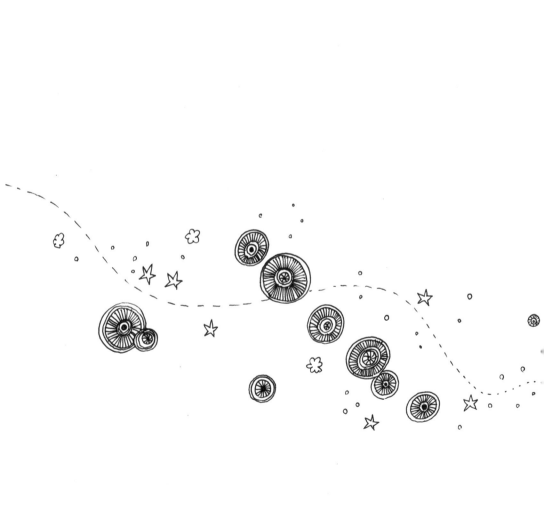

HELP! FASHION EMERGENCY!
I don't know what to wear.
your presence is required immediately.

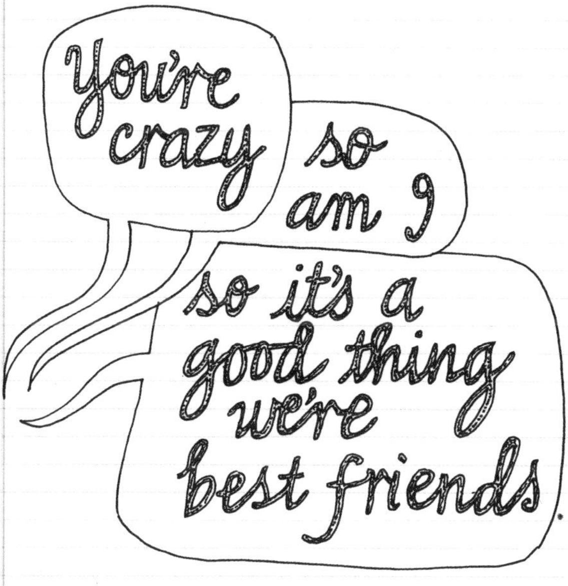
You're crazy
so am I
so it's a good thing we're best friends.

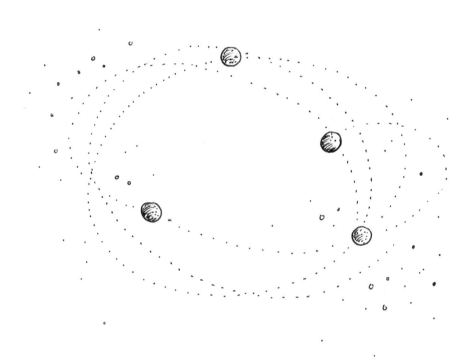

if I ever get asked
to lead a space voyage
to the moon, I promise
that I will take you
with me. In the meantime,
we can sit on the roof
and gaze at the stars.

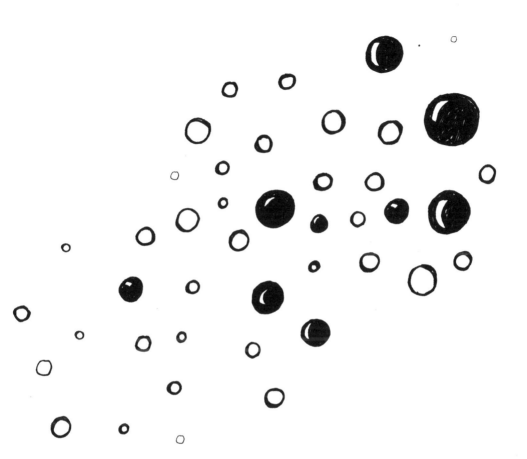

I'M WRITING TO INFORM YOU
THAT WE ARE NOW OVERDUE
FOR A LONG CHAT.
I HAVE SO MUCH TO TELL YOU...

the other day
on the street I passed
2 girls laughing
with abandon, and it
reminded me of us.
(of course they were wearing good shoes...)

there is
always a
cup of tea
waiting for you
at my
table...

ISBN 978-1-74270-057-1

Produced and originated by PQ Blackwell Limited
116 Symonds Street, Auckland, New Zealand
www.pqblackwell.com

Published in 2011 by
Hardie Grant Books
85 High Street
Prahran, Victoria 3181, Australia
www.hardiegrant.com.au

Copyright © 2011 PQ Blackwell Limited

Illustrations by Carla Shale
Quote research and creation by Rachel Clare
Book design by Cameron Gibb and Sarah Anderson
Photograph acknowledgements are as follows: pp. 9, 15, 23, 27, 35, 43, 47, 51, 57 and 63 by Jacqui Blanchard; pp. 5,
11, 13, 16, 19, 24–25, 31, 32–33, 39, 48–49 and 52 by Carla Shale; front and back cover and pp. 6, 7, 10, 17, 36, 37,
40, 41, 45, 53, 55, 58, 60 and 61 by iStockphoto; pp. 28–29 by PQ Blackwell.

The publisher is grateful for literary permissions to reproduce items subject to copyright. Every effort has been
made to trace the copyright holders and the publisher apologises for any unintentional omission. We would
be pleased to hear from any not acknowledged and undertake to make all reasonable efforts to include the
appropriate acknowledgement in any subsequent editions.

'The path is not straight. Mistakes need not be fatal' used with permission of Marion Winik.

Printed in China